COOL COLORING

FOR
kids

Express Yourself Through Color

STERLING CHILDREN'S BOOKS
New York

D0879348

STERLING CHILDREN'S BOOKS
New York

An Imprint of Sterling Publishing
1166 Avenue of the Americas
New York, NY 10036

First Sterling edition published in 2016.
First published in Great Britain in 2015 by Buster Books,
An imprint of Michael O'Mara Books Limited,
9 Lion Yard, Tremadoc Road, London SW4 7NQ
www.busterbooks.co.uk

© 2015 by Buster Books

Illustrations by Chellie Carroll, Fay Martin, Felicity French, and Jane Hayes
Written and edited by Lauren Farnsworth
Designed by Jack Clucas
Cover designed by Angie Allison
With additional material provided by Shutterstock

ISBN 978-1-4549-2053-3

Distributed in Canada by Sterling Publishing
c/o Canadian Manda Group, 664 Annette Street
Toronto, Ontario, Canada M6S 2C8

For information about custom editions, special sales, and premium and
corporate purchases, please contact Sterling Special Sales at 800-805-5489
or specialsales@sterlingpublishing.com.

Manufactured in China
Lot #:
2 4 6 8 10 9 7 5 3 1
05/16

www.sterlingpublishing.com

Coloring is a great creative way to relax and have fun! With a combination of coloring and doodling pages, this book is sure to fuel your inner artist. You can use any shade, pattern, and design that you like. And don't worry about staying inside the lines!

Different colors can make you feel different things. Blues and green can make you feel tranquil, like you are sailing on an ocean. Reds and oranges can make you feel strong and energetic, like you are hiking on a sunny day. Mix and match your favorite colors to create your own cool image and bring your own flair to the pages!

RED

Red is courageous.
This energetic, bold color
can make you feel fiery
and strong.

ORANGE

Orange is daring. This warm and glowing color can make you feel eager and determined.

YELLOW

Yellow is joyful. This bright and sunny color can make you feel smiley and cheerful.

GREEN

Green is peaceful. This calm and soothing color can make you feel refreshed.

BLUE

Blue is calm. This tranquil and peaceful color can make you feel relaxed.

PURPLE
Purple is majestic. This rich and grand color can make you feel regal.

PINK

Pink is shy. This delicate and
blushing color can make you
feel quiet and soft.

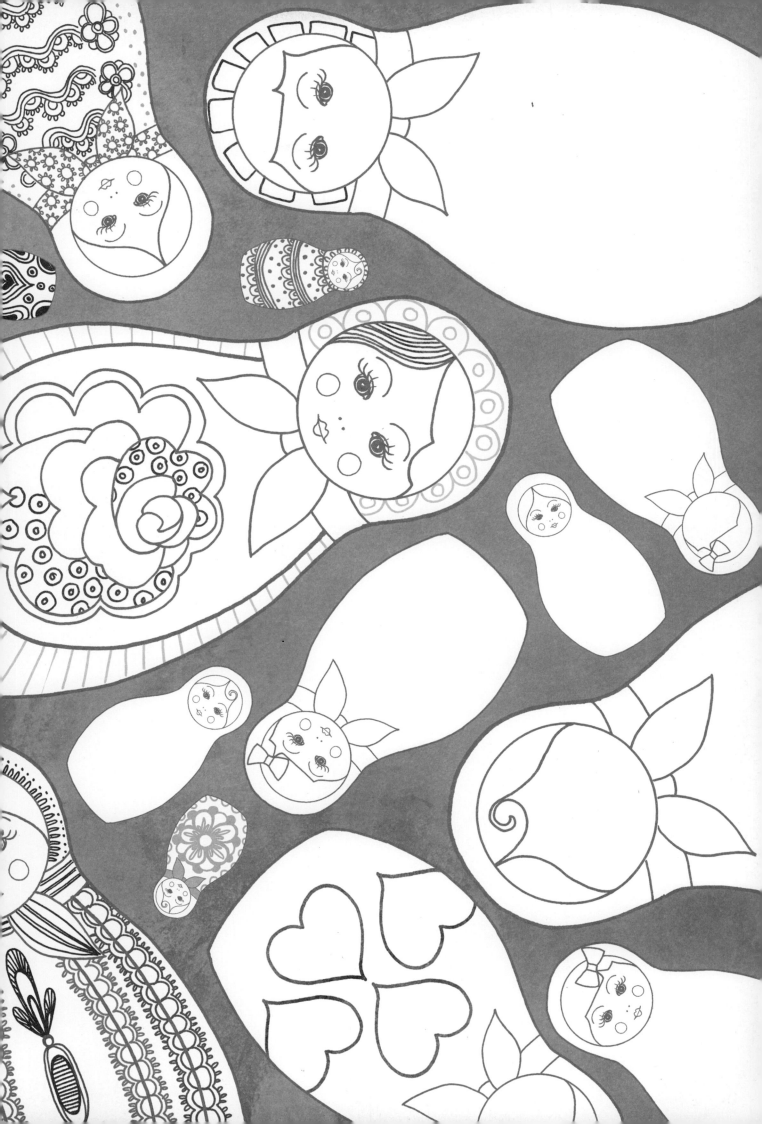

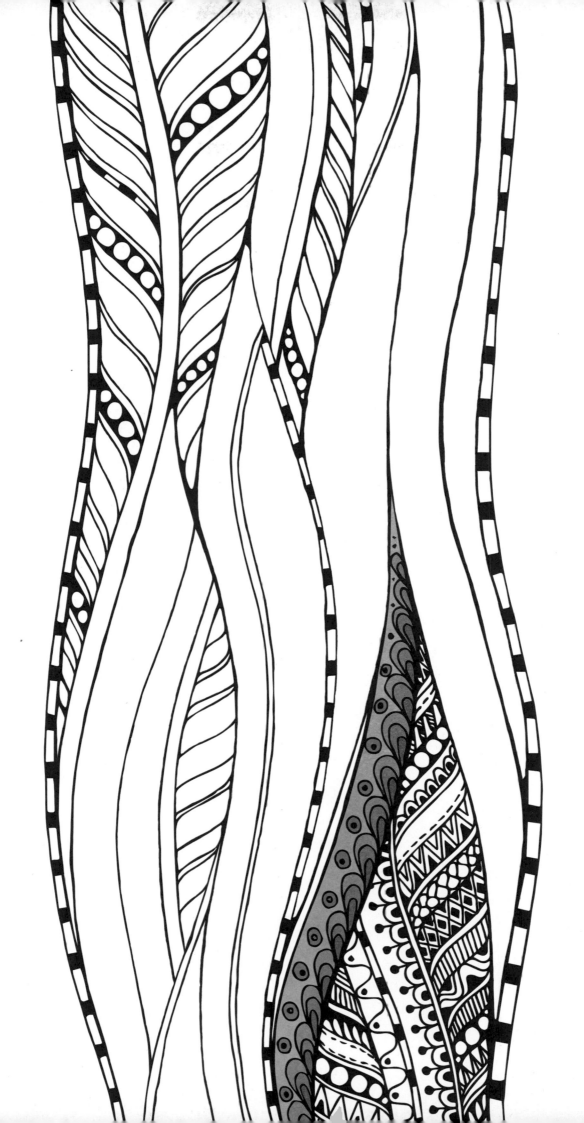

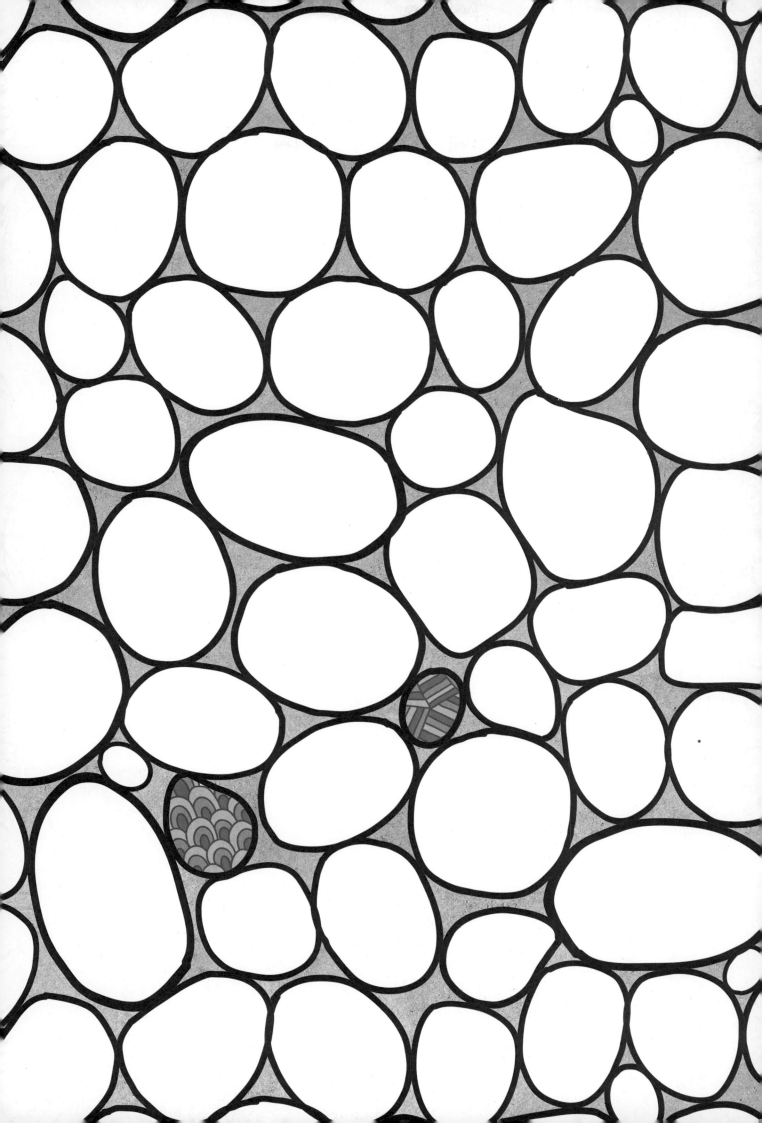

BLACK

Black is secretive. This dark and mysterious color can also be filled with brightness and light.